MW01503513

OrangeBooks Publication

Smriti Nagar, Bhilai, Chhattisgarh - 490020

Website: **www.orangebooks.in**

First Edition, 2022

ISBN: 978-93-5621-081-3

OTHER SIDE OF THE LAST HILL

PARTHITA DUTTA

OrangeBooks Publication
www.orangebooks.in

INTRODUCTION

In my first book, 'The Boatman Beckons,' I tried to covey through a hundred poems of light, hope, and light, that everything is not over; there is still a new day, there is rain, and there is life, only when the perspective changes, the hope wakes up again.

'Other Side of The Last Hill' is my second book of poetry. In my first book where I ended, I have started from there, and gone deeper into intricacies this time. I have tried to give life through the interplay of diction and rhythm to the thousand floating thoughts like clouds of every mind, that come and go unnoticed, unveiling the severe impacts of common words born out of it. The metaphoric nature of Poetry and its rhythmic beauty, and symphony is always my first choice as a literary tool whenever I compose my thoughts into a literary craft; and open verse gives me more freedom to fondle with my thoughts.

Our life is a tale of words of excitement; besides word being sound, it also evokes emotions that give shape to life. Love is the breath of life. Hence, it is the secret of creation; if one wants to taste it, one must see the goodness of things.

I have tried to take such ideas to the depth of the reader's mind with the ornaments of poetry and nature. I hope I will succeed.

Author: Parthita Dutta

FOREWORD

Recommending Parthita Dutta 's "Other Side of The Last Hill"

A Recommendation is a suggestion or proposal as to the best course of action advised or items to be selected, especially one put forward by an authoritative person or body. I am a lover of poetry and I therefore, recommend Parthita Dutta's "Other Side of The Last Hill"!

A poetry lover may well ask how brave should one be to recommend this intelligence in poetry. Let me give you a reason: As with all poetry, it has always been there, present, but unseen and only clarified in the form in which it presents itself to the poet's reader. And perhaps the most obvious universal quality of poetry in all languages is its form. It is the excellence of form in poetry that recommends itself to the reader. It is in the poem itself where we often find what we overlooked in the mastery of the beauty it brings.

Reading, yes, this is the most objective way to speak of it but you should never forget that to partake of that poetic form is the pleasure that invest in the human mind the quality that all humans share: The beautiful transformation of the hidden or concealed obvious made real.

I think this is why we come to poetry: To discover what we knew all along but needed this poet's discovery to see it clearly and see it revealed to us, her reader.

Parthita Dutta is a poet of learning and grace in two languages: Bengali and English, so beautifully expressed.

If philosophy is the wonder of reason, poetry is the wonder of language. This is why I recommend Parthita Dutta's book of poetry.

Stephen W COLE
June 7, 2022
Overland Park, Kansas USA

INDEX

Chapter – 4: Live And Love 173

CHAPTER - 1: THOUGHTS

FALCON HEIGHT

On the white page, what have I
Today to give you more
Is it the art of poetry from a poet!
Is it a life route to change the ill fate!
Is it a knock to open the heavenly gate!

In a poetic wave,
A tuft of tale for everyday life
I will pour in your empty chalice…

It will travel through the eyes
Like an array of learned words
And like your essence
Will remain in concordance.

Leaving the jewels, and joy behind
I have gone deeper alone
To upturn every stone
In the dingy lane of the city
In the dense forest of empathy
In the nook of the house old
In the mangrove of the soul.

Are you now drooping yet thriving
Like an indoor plant on a pot,
With a little bit of abrupt shower!

I came as a boatman once
And beckoned you to the rising river
Did you find the answer to the quest!

This time, I will give you a falcon height
To aspire and determine with grace
For your destiny, the path, and pace.

FOOTSTEPS

After a while, the darkness will fade
And disappear.
After a while, the heavy rain will come to a halt
And smooth the front street.
After a while, the summer being vapour
Will depart. The cold wind
Through the course of the fountain
Will descend and touch
The feathery leaves of Poplar.

Going two steps forward
With little more spur
If you open the window by the head...
If you cease the anomalous, arbitrary sight
Fallen on the eyes at the door of the moment
Even the daily dissonant cry of gloom
In the heart, will play
The classical tune in the string of the Sitar.

Listen to the footsteps deep; he walks gently
On the green grass, thirst soaked in dew.

As sleep comes leaden heavy on the eyelids
That's how he will descend into the core of your heart
Embrace him, offering everything.

IN EVERY BENT OF THE WAY

In every bent of the way
I meet a lonely soul cursing his mate
With lists of adventures.
I pause to light and show him
The eastward road to the sun
No, no, from here, you must walk alone
I want nothing of your jewels
Instead, I cast off my coat and confectionaries
For I will roam long to reach home.

Oh, Lord, this world, and its ways
Understands only the worth of money
Not the metaphor of my sore sigh
I don't want this lurid gold wreath
To confiscate my free will
But the handful of pearl yielded
I will give you all, by and by.

Till your tongue says, enough
You will double the thirst, be it the hate or lust
My road is quaint, and I find joy
Walking home with defeat and pain
I am wealthy, whole in my spirit
I don't want anything from your world
I don't want anything that you sell.

IF YOU ALLOW

It's not mystic,
Not an intricate lore
You, in your being
Are happening, unsure.

An impregnated lotus
Sleeping unborn
In the hidden core
Of your dwindling heart.

An orb of fire
Like an impregnated star
Eclipsed by the futility
In the centre of your eyes.

There is a boiling passion
Intercepted spark
Wrought in your fabric
Yet not claimed or uncovered.

To your God, you chant as if a ritual
That you desire to live in the stream of joy
That you desire to love in requital of love
Only then your hands are unfurled outward
At other times they are stiff, fisted
And your legs are vine and lumbered
Hence the robe of perception
Seems falling on you like hell.

To the hundred losers if you listen in fear
That no matter how you try
One more time, you will lose and go down
To the forlorn queue. You won't know
That you are born of a decree
To adhere to a different path
That's walked by none before.

You don't know me; I have known you for long
If you allow, I will show you the unseen
A life rare and tranquil that exists in silence
On the other side of the hill, obscure
Across the river on the far shore
We will discover life in its shadow.

OTHER SIDE OF THE LAST HILL

Many times, I have gone further
Having lost in the half-light
Into the green woods
Camouflaged, in the crowd of mortals
To be bright.

And there, the varnished days
Of the royal tapestry
Shall build
My paradise on earth.

But the gushing waves of epoch
Wrecks the pillars of oyster-dreams
Futile trough of failure, ferments
When the bottom sand slides.

Though an uninterrupted lucidity
Cleanses darkened pores
Where neither remains longing
Nor loathing, as long
As I hold the ocean
Within my lacrimal glands.

O my master,
In silent tongue tell me
By which anchor
You drag me to your feet,
And awaken a Bodhisattva!

Would you hint me
My harbour for a shift
In silent tongue…

Yet again, bubbles form in strata
And the conviction returns
In breathing and belief
Where through the half-light,
I walk a little further
To the other side
Of the last hill, to build
My paradise on earth.

IF YOUR EYES BERTH ON MY VERSES

O dear, perchance
If your eyes berth on my verses,
Try the beauty of life one more time.

Feel the richness in your heart
That rhythmic beat
In the yearning for love.

Other than the shadow of guilt,
Yesterday is a memory
That recollects the traces, you see.

Other than the apprehension
Of uncertainty,
Tomorrow is imaginary, you see.

Look up, isn't the clear sky
Telling you something-
To be free, to be at ease!

There is no cloud today to obstruct
The ardour and the zeal
That you seek in frenzy, all around
Everything is sunflower bright
My limbs are airy, my heart blows
With the wind that carries the world:
Today singing in joy, "let's be merry."

The road which is exhausted other days
From overload, looks carefree.
The warbling of the Nightingale and Robin
Like an orchestra, subdue the noise
Of the lunatics and the factory.
You, me, and life in service, together
Can define joy as inner and sublime.
O dear, today, let's live in the whole sphere.

THE SUN SHALL RETURN

My beloved Blueberry lost heart
Last year in stark grey winter
Exposing gaunt juiceless limbs,
Withered and faced death.
Everyone perceived it died,
But I deferred the ritual for a year,
Could not cremate my desire
To see the berry bubbling.

Thought I: 'let it stand like an abstract tree
Till my mind strays in southward wind.
By then, the earth had finished
A year of pilgrimage,
Brought the threshold benedictions,
And out of the arid body
Life sprouted like clove plumes.
Months later,
There were hanging berries.

I still wonder how Trout and Bluegills
Under the frozen layers,
Build a warm sunken island
For the sore sea!

From the backseat, I observed,
Dinu and Mirza laugh like crackers
Pulling rickshaw on hot cauldron path.
Drops of sweat fall on folklore lips
The wheel drives half a dozen children's whim
and is born a new mosquito maggot dream.

Night Jasmine waits firmly, the sun
Shall return from the neighbour's door.
Till then, the city lights may wear
The crown of glory
Do you think life ever dies!
One dies when death takes the life away
Thus they live, smile, and return
To the same story.

I WALK IN DISCIPLINE

I walk in discipline
In the discipline of ants' queue, I walk along.
In the marathon of countless overweening people
As the night deepens, asthma worsens.

They are darting for a threshold of any kind
Running blindfolded in all directions
Just like before the sign of a storm.
Young adults refer to this as speed.

Breaking all established rules
Is no longer an easy task in middle age.
Laws of the earth, constitutions, societies,
And the laws set by you...

There are fewer hazards if bowed to the laws.
But standing quietly, I too break sometimes.

I have applauded your success and felt good.
I'm fine, burning and dying amid billion stars,
Knowing not if I were a star or the dust.

There must be a ground-breaking love,
To be the pole star in your eyes,
So let me decorate you as you desire.

In your eyes, so many butterflies, elevation,
Forest of beauties.
I'm fine; a drop in the ocean of people, floating
Like clear water vapour. You will be well.
Remember to get one full wave across,
The loss comes after the gain.

YOU FAIL TO UNDERSTAND

Have you ever flipped a fallen leaf or a fallen letter
And noticed, was there anything written under?
Have you ever fixed your eyes on the moving lips
And hearkened words that were never released?
Have you ever, in repetition, read an inscrutable text
And perplexed, why every time
It did reveal a new meaning!
Have you ever touched a wild wayside plant,
And felt akin, but to others
Could not express in words?
Have you ever doubted your biased vision
That cannot transcend an opaque body?
It is not a mere theory that, under the surface
To shield are n number of layers there
Even though you don't see all things,
Still, they exist and multiplying
Even though something is unknown to you
But they are happening within your reach
For your own reason,

You fail to understand the extremities
That the grief doesn't befall only to break thee
That the tear doesn't flow only to flood your will
That the joy doesn't come to let you carefree.

STORM MOUNTS

Even that day, there was a storm
In the carnival
When all were revelling
In an eye wink, the Shamiana blew off
Like a soldier, we fought
The harsh wind.

The storm mounts, ripping the ocean:
Like a tower of despair
On the temples
When deluge discomfort raises
Every spectator passes by
With a cold nonchalance.

The hollow plates bang in chorus,
In the song of starvation, the house flies dance
Far-off wine, pork, and cherry
Is decked and dangled
On an affluent eventide
Of flirtation
And rain of currency.

Near the equator, there
Looms the black smoke of disparity,
Develops a tornado arm.

When lights of jubilation veil the emanating star,
Descends darkness
On the roofs of a forgotten town,
The chimney sobs dense clouds
Then depression breaks into the rain
Even that day, there was a storm.

COMET QUERIES

The tarnished promises
The unanswered comet queries
Had shattered as dust
At the turbine wheels
In the desert yard of life.
Flipping the heap
Of dry leaves and scraps,
I never looked for them,
They're the buried burden.
For I trust my love was genuine
And the firefly still shining
In a vial kept years
At a secret cellar.

One day maybe
A wrong turn might bring
You to my door
When you will be weary
Of spreadsheet society
And caustic concocted lie
The time will cease
Into an eternal evening.

ANXIETY

In the steep inlet of survival test
The overwhelmed reason
Jams the canal of the brain
Like a shipwreck, dead-deafen self
I billow between the two limbs
Of losing and winning.

Why do the thoughts go wild
Then twist, and wrench the sinews
By the wheezing siren
Of the imminent rumoured train
At my covenant dawn!

Though I know even the valorous king
Ere the day of battle stood fixed
By the bevelled windowpane
To foresee the fate
With a thumping heart rate,
Yet my breath
Billows between the two limbs
Of losing and winning.

When the larva bursts
Out of my chest
I am on the verge of losing
The leg doesn't stay on a spot
Anxious: Will he come today?

CONTOUR

Still the moth orchid is alive
It's not that long past
As the memory has no dust
Yet the portrait is sketchy.

How fondly I used to twine
With the tweeting ladies of the spring!
We dissected the weather, recipe,
Trend, and the man we love.

Without a thud like a wight
Born my inner-conscious
A judge with a gavel bottled me
Cramming me in the guilt, a brine
Of critical connotations of time.

Being defiant like a squirrel
I fought, but not long then
Cringed, as nothing was stored
But a hollow of husk talks.
We reconciled, and it got the reign.
One day:

In the chromosomes of a poet
I heard a Philomel whistling
I was aspired to write the lyrics
Of oceanic emotions and grief
From the contour of gibberish.

I CAME TIME AND AGAIN

When you were drenching
Dolefully in the rain of despair,
That day as a mote of peace
In the white pigeon's beak, I came
And you were struck, spoiled
By the feather again
There, I melted on her tongue.

When you were breaking
In the clamorous ravine,
Between the heart and life
In the grip of solitude appeared I
And you got ghastly terrified
Of your inner silence
There the crowd swallowed me.

When your cogency became supine
By numerous tyrant blows
You groped for an imperial spire,
Being a spark of Tanzanite
I fell on your diadem as a light
Nonchalantly you breathed me out.

BLISS

Did you ever touch or feel
The subtle body of bliss?
Observe those who look
Calm and complete.

Like I met a wintry furry cat
On the bench, lying tamed-
Closed eyes, whiskers
Downed in delight,
And the body pulsated
In the quilt of sunlight,
Curled in a wimple of bliss.

Like the sleeping infant
On the mother's warm lap,
Nonchalant, a heavenly scene
Connecting all realms divine
And the baby breathes in bliss.

It is a state where you see
No wrinkles of worry,
No frets of fear,
No ruckus of restlessness,
A slope to slide unto the stillness
By tossing the time and tomorrow
As the engrossed ocean in a droplet
There emerges a halo of bliss.

I MAY

I am a hollowed headspace
Like a cemetery cypress
Whenever I finish a verse.

I am a frantic aspirant
Often suffer a vertigo
In the middle of the trail.

You're so quiet, deathlike
My tiny wit is drying out
If you sense my receding pulse
And unmoved lips
Let me have your mercy.

Let my sight innately linear
I may read the symbols
The clouds are typing
On the void cyan face.

Let my mind fathom the jolt
That forms the spindrift
I may hear the unvoiced speech
As ultrasound vibrato lyrics.
Let the satin fly off the coffin
I may see another realm
Where the soul rests in peace
I may, and I may, I may…

REALITY

Of divine warmth in His palms
Shaped the unparalleled living planet,
Outpouring promise, a garden of Eden.

Abundant greenfield, erect trees,
River-sea-flower-fruits fascinating
Sedate calm shadows as offerings.

When the bright star shakes off some dust,
You and I wake up in the flesh as being,
A timely phenomenon, for what?

A bestowed benediction to love and praise
The laurels with a free will, animals, and birds
Are to witness us, a precedent of nature's law.

We love till each cell of the body is brought close
Enough to create a replication, insuperable fact.

Where have we been mistaken then?
In the pith of the progeny
There is seen workshop of hatred and rage
And madness for retaliation.

From east to west in the brazen light
Unuttered is jeopardy and privation.

Still, there grows red rose, carnation, and tulip
Sporadically, do you have any choice but love?

AS DAWN

A day wakes up from the womb, seemingly
Bathes in ceremonial dew, fringed
With white scented plumeria, unwinds
Its disc from glorious yellow
To pure white in elements.

On her wide plane hits
Several rainstorms, fumes of wildfire,
Upheavals, and outrage,
Shakes not or deter from her heights.

Her mythical magic adds colours
At best to every sphere of forms, mandala décor,
An orchestra at play, what we call 'lively.'

Till she reaches the overhead sun,
Carries the flurry trail longer, wider, larger
The noontide, a time
To repose and reflect within.

Her soul is separate from the illusion
By a deep gorge of truth
Thus, she propagates to the darkness,
A dense blanket and she dissipates like a solvent
In the vermillion twilight
And never seen shrieked for death.

I wish ere I had realized
That we are born as dawn
To rise like a day.

GULMOHAR WISH

This is how some archaic
And medieval flyers float
In the solitary bay, every day.

The preachers and philosophers,
The noise on dusty path ajar,
The tulip face, heart burst laughter,
The muffled groan whacking from
The other side of the shared wall
Even the scattered guilt and folly
Shows up unhindered.

Sometimes, like a sunbeam spear
You enter with the bulk affairs
And stay a little, in my head.

In memory, it's easy
To hold your hand. Stained glass
Gives a wrong notion of life.
But I am placid and clear in my ethics
With the confessions delivered
Of my part, the error, and impatience.

All your partiality, prejudice, perversion
I forgave. I closed my account, know this.

Know this, the Gulmohar tree still flowers
Dark red like before, as we wished.

SAFFRON

In the deluge of emotion, I found myself
Sinking like a small stone in deep water
The only consolation was
That I could sense your agony.

When I urge an expansion, why
Would I subtract or divide
To be the smaller unit, though
I sever my unseen importune heads
That growl, yell, grumble, and scream.

I feel a profound peace to aver
That I can love even in extreme antagonism.

Care is a concern, and concern shapes love.
How the care hinges a leaf to the stem, likewise
You and I, bound with one central cord.

When one stirs, the other feels the quake
And tension builds.
You never know when that concern
Turns a fear or anxiety
But you feel, love is a severe pain
Where one must duck and mould
For the attainment and the stiffest task
Is to shift the focus from the self.

Have you known about the ascetic path,
Where one detaches from his kinsman
But attaches painstakingly to the unknown
To be free from bondage?
But in the wordless realm, who will tell, how!

Have you seen those who wear saffron
And sit years by the riverbank,
To tell us or to tell himself
That he detached from all!
They hide the answer in the heap
Of dun matted hair, secured
In a coil on the top of his head.

I could see, at least, that it absorbs
The city's dust.
Why do they blow smoke?
What still bothers them, the body?
I came to know saffron symbolizes
The colour of dawn and dusk
Perhaps, I understand the philosophy.

I AM A SOLDIER

For a fleeting time, I am an ultima sky
By ornamenting me with the stars gifted by you.
They depart one by one in the depth of night.

The cohort chaos, the applauds,
The choir of praise, the inherited fate,
The contemporary trend under the spotlight
Muffles the euphony of the humble bird
And the hymns of the Holy Gita.

From the lump of loam, I stood up
As if a man, nothing to think
Twice and confirm
I am a soldier of the Crusade.
I am a baton of nonviolence
In the likely independence.

Many times, I am half asleep and listen
To my soul speaking:
"If you choose today, do it right away."

I will give my last drop of spirit
To change your view,
Want nothing in return. You will admit
That heaven is there,
Where you were bequeathed a life.
Yes, you may say this is
My venturesome audacity.

I HEAR THE CRY

I hear the cry of the tender grass
When you clip them for mowing a lawn.
I hear the possibility of ties
That tear and fall under your feet.

Two men of eccentric taste
Will be coming nigh
For a ritualistic affair ever.

Unsurpassable ups and downs seracs
Will remain in between
To distinguish them, as two men,
Yet two men will come nigh.

The green bile of your sentiments
That ooze to sabotage attempts
Of building the desired bonding
Has burnt me anyway.

Who are you behind the attire?
A steep and stony sculpture
That condescends
And overpowers everything
That intends to blend in uniformity!

You don't know
How I dwindle in dejection
Failing from planting
One more mustard seed
By a Godly kiss from my soul.

There are a few who comes to earth
As Seraph, on the thorny path
To tug the wheel by an inch
And depart without a sigh.

OBLIVION

When an ink-filled pen is driven
By the twitch of grief, anguish, and hope
The diction dances with the meter
And plays a rhythm on my soul.

When a thoughtful brush sways
Right and left, north and south, and
Everywhere splashes the fervid passion
Even an obscure painting speaks
The language of my soul.

When the pressing hands fondly caress
A lump of clay, carve a piece
Of wood or stone, even
A lifeless statue express, protests,
Celebrates through my soul.

When the fingers stroke, fiddle
On the strings, a tempo
Falls and rises in harmony
That prod, and incise the pure essence
Of melancholy in my soul.

In oblivion, he, who
Worships the elements
Emulating the image of what exists
And what exists not,
Will be elevated with certitude
In the eye of God.

SPACE

Among the hundred things I ventured
I am winning in one, knowing you more than you do.

I am peacefully pouring my life into yours
And I have known that there's a pathless valley
Perpetual between us, defined by
Birth calendar, for good. That we call space.

You must understand that space
Between the two wombs that deliver us
Between two different arrangements of stars
Between two different senses and genitals
That space is lying peacefully undisturbed.

You see, maybe that is the reason
While we were waving at the shore
Three different waves striving, you, me, and the sea.
From the ardent union born several cacti
Hence there was the restlessness by the dusk.

Perhaps you will never know that space

For it awakes when all sleep by the night

That space is good, and we are drawn closer to the light

Maybe the bat or the owl has seen the figure of it.

WHEN THE WAITING ENDS

When the waiting ends, there
You are, with the absence of waiting
The unceasing numbers in the head
And thus, you perish.

They clink, squabble, possess, and hold
They are the colour bids of a necklace
They are the character of the tale
Or else there is no tale to tell.

If I ignore the temper and tone
Like few peals of thunder but lots of rain
They are worthwhile; they are real
And they are the tremor
That awakens the hill.

When I open the door, one will enter
To end the wait, one will speak
And the torpidity break.

What is there in a moderate
World of mine, the rim of papers
That deaf upholstery, and fellow men
To whom I am a foreign threat!

Though I learn from nature
Yet I fail to fathom if I may sustain
Being a winter tree, bereft
Of the foliage and fruits
How will I stand so artistic?

EMPHASIS ON MIND

I didn't weave a garland other than
A garland of words.
The flower which belonged to the tree, the tree
That belonged to the garden, the garden that
Belonged to someone else's estate, was
Beyond my reach.

One big house around the globe
In the city of my thought, I build
Every day. The brick and stone all break
Everything is sand, friable
Everything collapses in a slight tremor.

Even though I came close to you
Couldn't touch the questions on your lips.
I am searching for the meaning
In the meaningless heaps.

Yet if you meet the answer,
Would you build the habitable world
Without taking anything in return?

I have high faith
Like the fall of a temporal apple
In the eyes of Newton
The hidden mysteries
Will reveal to the seeker.

With the thread of my body
If I could make a spider net,
I ponder deep, what's impossible!
What's impossible if I search
For the extraordinary in general.

SOMETIMES

For something that day
The sky hid her face for long
By a thick blanket of grey.

For something that day
The sea was calm, disheartened
Though the waves had frills
But weren't that gay.

To sing along with the seashore
The people who came,
The sudden damp, cold spray
Made them onto disarray.

But a flock of white swans
In circles, was showing pomp
With their royal wings, they knew
That people were there
To catch the beauty,
And I asked one:

"Dear, why do all seem gloom today?"
And it answered promptly: "Sometimes,
Living among man,
They too become humanely."

SUPERLATIVE

You, who are so great
In wealth, power, and lineage
Is surpassing, superlative.
I or like mine standing spartan
For many years at the side
Of the field and farm
In between, there is-
An unsurpassable distance.

O, notable!
Yet I will say, you got wrong
The grandiose in your throne
Is not the respect or love,
It is the brewed fear
On the face
Of uncounted commoners
Like me or mine.

If you descend and stand abreast
Taking off the mask of name, fame, and glory
And open your heart, you would see
Those who strive to survive in life
Their simple love is the greatest treasure
That they carry to the last ritual.

Whenever I look up, the open sky
Embark on my chest, perfumed air
Sway my flickering hope
And the soil...
I never measure its height
Yet so close, so great, so glorious.

You have grown a high head
But not glorious.
No one is venerable now,
One has to be a pioneer to be that.

LETTER

I left it written, believe me
Everything else I wanted in this life
I didn't want enmity, didn't want barbed wire,
Didn't want superiority.
How many times in the wind letter
With the softness of the dawn, I said
No self-interest, no fear of night
Just let love, else leave in the afternoon
Or evening to another land.
Alas, anything that is easily found
Has it ever had a price! Outdated Dime.
Sitting on a banyan altar
Since I could not say the ancient words
Mixing with the metal,
They perished as undesirable.
Yet I am not surprised.

You play 'round the world', in the light of ignorance.

When you did not put my name in the manuscript of life

Don't ever call that name posthumous

In the mirror of memory, there is no death

Of the soul, do not wake him again

On the stage of the world, will suffer greatly.

CHANCE

In the barren incandescent eve
Let me sing my Ujjain lore
Of miracles and mysteries
To melt the frosted precipice.

Let me reminisce in an eye wink
What brought us together,
In this strangely arable brink
Where we bleed silently
For plenty of reasons
Of the parapet possession.

Hadn't our arbour blown away
By the blustery expectation
And bulge dejection of acquisition
We would've known,
Our brief acquaintance
Is not by unknown stumble
But by the blueprint
Of patterned chance.

CHAPTER - 2: VISION

BLOOM POETIC

...And my gaze wanders
Through the advent
Of spring, like the pollinators
In search of iridescence,
That temp.

A sublimity showering
Like golden confetti
Wherever focus shifts.

Nature's abundance,
Supreme promise
In flora and fauna
That overwhelms
Yet seems tantalizing.

The earth whispers
Secretly…
It is the time
To mate, to breed,
To make love befit
The heart sings:
O, magnolia…
Make them love,
Bloom profuse,
Bloom poetic.

I OBSERVE

His one amorous stroke
Impregnates the blank sky
With fascinating hues.

The crimson carnation
Allures purple evening
Uniting in Prussian blue.

His water brush draws
The mirror for the sky.
The vast lake beneath captures
The continuum
On its refractive surface
In deepening silence
I observe.

One more stroke enlivens
The ambitious canvas
The perennial pasture, hedgerow
With wild grass and blossoms
Enamour the pollinators.

And they fly for a purpose
With inherited wings,
In all tracks, connecting
Painted objects ideally
I observe.

Like that rigid mountain
Inertly waiting
Behind the veil,
I observe.

The dynamic landscape
Moves forth,
Like floating clouds, moves forth.
I am waiting for His one last stroke
Which would tell me
Where do I stand!

POETRY AWAKES

When silence deepens
In the stillness of the night
When varied words dance
As of snowflake's flight
When emotions drip as blood
In the wound of thorny red rose
When the moon heart melts
In the silvery soul's expose
Trades and exchanges are over
Choices and urges are sober
Thence, one meets the self
In an elfish onyx glen
Where poetry awakes
In the bosom of a lone star
Across the expanse of the azure
Whispers a twitching passion
And rain of poetry exudes
Through the vigorous veins.

DEEP LAKE

Beneath your arch eyebrow
Is a leaf-shaped deep lake,
I am yet to know the depth,
Rowing my boat, equipped.

Your throbbing breath
Is sending ripples of urge
To be together, to listen
To each other patiently.

It could be midnight
But I shall anchor soon
Let the beacon burn
On your bow lips to lead me
To the panorama port.

Blink not, stay by the door
In the shrine of the seraglio,
I shall adorn and worship
All your treasured feelings.

MEETING STILLNESS

The mind is restless
As long as the electrons run
In a lower orbit the stability comes
And fluctuates again

It was fun, feign to be free
As if water, liberated into vapour
Of the lonely day,
The shore evermore, feels
Like a desolated castle

Hearken, hearken between
The tone of morn and eve
There's a perdurable noontide
The grief from the joy is apart
By the sinusoid trough and crest

There is a coiled Sheshnag,
Where the stillness reinforcing
Behind fleeting, hung clouds
Is a solemn still sky, manifesting

Under the soaring roaring waves
A mass of still water, concentrating
Amidst the creaking, rustling din
The soul of the still forest, meditating

Your laugh, cry, anger, and satire
Are like electrical impulses
Having no separate measures to me
The stillness is gripping and gripping.

TRANQUILITY

Today, I rise tranquil
Tying my tottering vision
From that, what is not done
Hushing all the concerns.

Today, the dawning sun
Soaks the Parijat's cassock
And she lays passionately
An orange-pedicled fate
On my white pilgrim path.

Today, the flute zephyr
Through the Neem branch
Cleanses long bitter bile
The thought vessel is now
Riddance of the virile.

Today, the blushing butterfly
Shows gratitude on the plate
They hover in the house,
Having found a vanguard leading
Ignoring yesterday's din,
Tranquil.

Hence today, I urge
To offload the haystack
To respite at the twilight nest
No fear of towering darkness
As no rift is felt between
Inhale and exhale; I close
The door today in tranquillity.

THE CAPTIVATING 'SHE'

How captivating she was
Alas! I couldn't hold her beauty!
On moments-
Greyish mica sand glittering
In glamourous moonlit streams

On moments-
Chronicle waves crashing
On the erect breast of the rocky cliff

On moments-
Serpent roads spring-loop
Around the green deciduous hill

Like glued mascara on eyelids
Only acquaintance,
And in the night, often wash away
By the Euphrates river's flow.

If I could meet her, a day
When far draws near on flashes,
On an evening portico
Earthen candlelit Basil stage,
Herd of cow returns homeward…
Flute symphony of Shephard…
Thatched roof, leafy curry
Iron pot-soaked fermented rice…
The sleep may embark.

In ambushed skinny crow eyes
If I meet her again in the lantern light,
I shall hold her firm, bind her beauty
Never, never let her go.

DUST

The dust that aggregates
By hill steps, head mounts
Like ages imperial Red Fort
Or tall upright transitory trunk
Of the Camphor tree and conqueror...

In the wave of time's bay
Same dust transform, gather
Grey layer in the yard alleys
On the sleek surface
Of Egypt tomb and properties
And heaps like deposited dirt
In the moist corner of my eye.

That dust, do you condemn, while
Cleaning it away from the day?

After touring Siberia, Sahara
Far beyond the farthest diaspora
Behind triviality and dullness,
Like bowed janitor and broom
My dime eyes have seen the merit
Those arthropods in a garbage pit

The consideration comes after the ruin
Dust born and dissolves into dust,
Source particles, quantum rain
Parts of God fall by grace, broken.

MERCY

Many winters, you've been
cold, impassive ruminating
of my medicinal goodness; this summer
before you get thawed and green
while tending the peony and poppy,
would you let me bloom, a bud
of mercy in your dooryard?

BALANCE

Look, the slim horizon is lying
Between the sky and the sea
And the birds to fly are free

Look, the mountain lifts the vale
As a monument to the summit
And silence rests on the peak

Look, the willows are drunk
In the song, the river murmuring
And gravel rolls along with the life

Look, the sun is happy, smiling
And gleaming in fatherly bliss
To see how his offspring live
In uninterrupted akin unity

Don't you forget, my child, that
Under the depth of starry night
And on the day bright, this earth
And the jewel has an equal share
As square feet of needs, so find
Balance in the journey for peace.

HONESTY

Today the sun was glum, head hung
Like the baby, hushed up by rebuff
And nature was raining languor
Since morning, the teary landscape
A dripping medley that sang:
The tale of how she waves the sea
Fleets the sky floating a while and fall
To where she begets her identity
Monochrome honesty detains me.
I remain far from false fabrication:
The doctrine, a prosthetic leg of the chair
And the cameo promises which
Evaporates in stringent time.

PAINT A LIFE

Have you ever painted a life of pride?
On the bare canvas of the day,
Throw sprinkles: red, green blue
In symmetry, projecting mercy, humility, and grace.
See, the painting drawn by you is a paradise.
Wherein, abstract and figure comes in cohesion.
That life renews, and spring comes,
Stretches of the garden of flowers,
Only for you, or else
Who will worship the beauty?

AWESTRUCK

It was the brightest day, pixel rich
Brambleberry and blue were not scanty
And there she was, centre subject
Unknown of her bucolic beauty.

While rearing the saplings
Her waist arched down. At an angle
Her body bent as if a tent in the field.

Legs covered with soft lulling sludge
Anchored and raiment, red hem
Secured in folds above the knee.

With a flat spatula, the olive sun
Greased her skin stainless, the sweat
Paced in branches like the brook
But eyes were veiled from the scene
Absorbed in weaving a presage.

And the wind teased her flirting,
The hairdo was undone and swayed
Streak by streak, not so far, a lark
Parched on a scarecrow, whistling
Knew not why, for an instant, all eyes
Beholding, were awestruck, reflecting
Was it the grace of nature or her!

REPELLING

Did you forget those days
Consonance, exfoliating talks
On the shore of noontide?

I put the devil to sleep
In the bolted cellar,
Singing angel and fairy
For you to spend hours savouring
Some cherry of pearly glee

Until the winter rested
I procured the wool
From the foraging sheep
And the warm apparel
Comforted you

Are you dreary now
That you chose
A dungeon over the day!

You see only craters
On the face of the full moon.
You see slag and cinders
In the fresh pulp of mid-June.

Your body mirrors in rose
You hate jasmine,
And I always smell it!

I am a faithful violet,
And you look better
In the molten fiery red.
Let us do part and disperse
As no longer, I esteem
Your fungal company.

COLORS

Her squishy oval cheek
Since morning was a mix
Of tamarind and pepper,
As the Warbler tweeted: the flurry
Of colours would cover all
The dead and dull yore days.

The most waited day poured
Jingling on her silvery anklet,
When the moist, mulberry mood
Formed an arch rainbow arbour
On her flowering fret.

She hid her face from coy
Nimbly behind the veil of fancy
Now and then, she paused
At her brewing beauty
On the mural mirror hanging.

Could she believe her own eyes
How her face adorned like Sri Radha,
Seeping dewy love for Krishna,
Who comes in the kingly chariot
Of golden day, and bathe her with
The shower of impending bliss.

She shut the subtle joy in her fist
When he held her hands tightly.
On her forehead, red sprinkles
He puffed! Then he slid his fingers
Through her green cherub cheeks.

Colours and colours, her body,
Yellow turmeric on the threshold,
The impressions remained forever
That she lived a day full of colours.

WINTER CANVAS

How far my eyes could capture
Is white and white, a few stripes
Of black and grey persist.
The riverbank turned white
By chilly crust like the frothy latex,
In pleat-by-pleat condensing
The worldly pain for a year.
The grey river streaming low
With arthritis in Aegean muse
Amidst the feathery fir.
Only the feathery fir, crowned
Of purity is grinning in green.
Towards the south, the sun
Began the journey to pacify
Devotees' yearning, as promised.
Over the horizon, his silhouette
Still present in orbed red
Says: "muse on my golden mirror
Till I come back soon."
In that quartz radiance, which
Reflects the rarest beauty of winter,
There, nature rests in an inner chamber

Day crawls on the clipped radius
And few lives quietly cleanse vices
On the holy fire burning
Unnoticed nearby somewhere.

SACRED MOTIF

We cleaned each corner nook,
Alcove cranny, and bay today
Of our life. Flayed the old fatigue
From the wall, wiped out the malevolence
From the windowpane, the furniture,
Fringed with floral frills, the house
Has dressed up as the new bride
Of festive joy and friendship in Diwali.

Bhoot, Preta, and Pishacha all
The dark shadows will hide or diffuse
For the veranda lanes have been lit up,
Flaming the purity and the goodness
In the heart. The green earth moulded
Into a golden orb, like a thousand sun
Radiating a lucid moonbeam
In the new moon night.

When the living souls, manifest
The sacred motif and luminosity of love,
Beauty exhibits the fruition of existence.

MY ANCESTOR

He gauged the sleeping waking
Of the sun and wind's warble
To fathom how rich would be
The moisture during the season.

He tilled, harrowed, levelled
To make sure the dormant life
Cosily wake in the soil bed.

He never got a bee-sting or
A viper bite, as he was the peer
They buzzed or hissed with.

Every night he slept on the
Trowel dream: weeding the day
And driving the locusts away.

His eyes awaited the time
Abounding with golden yields
Admiring a shovel, rake, and a hoe
The most precious thing he knew.

HOUSEMAID

Riding on a wheel of bustle
Her gait, as if she spins
The globe of the town.
She ignores inherited misfortune
And crushes it with her hard hoof
While trudging
And the allowance earned,
She keeps close to her heart
To build the castle in the air
Until she turns the doorbell on
The couple's knee won't work
The tea water won't boil
The marble floor won't get a polish
Near to ten minutes
Before she arrives, the clock
Slows and ticks louder
The elevator coop is affright
All rejoice the town gossip
From her plump cheek, though
Her leg cuff is deafening peal.

GENERATIONS

My grandma wishes as lief
A death, amid her folk in the countryside
Where her spirit would be lulled
By the air of Desho and Doab grass.
My mother moved to a town
Where the field yields factory for means.
She looks accomplished
Under the kitchen chimney and
Occasionally giggles, watching TV.
I imagined my palms holding
The whole earth studying, who runs it!
Hence, I moved across the continents,
Causing a painful elastic strain
In the pivot. My cult head
Trapped in the turban of India
And wanton feet tramping
On the geranium trails of Polska.

I see generations change
Perimeters
            And notions.
I didn't wonder that day when
My daughter stated: "I think
We ought to try living on Mars."

THE BENCH

From morning till twilight, the breeze,
And the larks, like a sound of a lute
Drift leisurely, somewhere nearby
Beside a lake, an empty wooden bench
Who made it? And for why?
Perhaps, it waits for kindred time!
If you be the next to rest, brief
As an exhausted comrade, you relive
The lemonade reverie as by many.
About the two-hand distance
A dishevelled leafy umbrella tree
With extended arms like an ally, usher
To a place where no one judges but
Listen to the thoughts go out as a sigh
There you unburden yesterday's injury
And tomorrow's trench, a light head, and body
Slouch like a vine. Instantly realize
Who holds you so firm and put forward:
Never mewling earth below the feet
And the never-shrinking sky above the chest.

WHEN SPRING ARRIVES

The warmth of the spring
Melts the ice and the numbness.
Water fills in the vernal pools
With grace and devotion
And the resurrection
Breaks the inertia finally.
The spring pours out
Meadows of new life, and plays
In forested visual.
The grinning of primroses
In hues by the alleys
The sensing of therapeutic grass
Under my feet
The white chariot of clouds
That floats in the poet's fancy
The metaphors are drawn
In bird's chirrup.

And the life merits, in inner nuances.
The expanse of mine, I see after
The riddance of all expenses
In the endless depth of the celestine.

UNTITLED

Down the years, there I was
A maiden fountain that streamed,
A monsoon cloud that roared,
A nifty sparrow that chirped
To the onlooker, it was
Overmuch, and unnecessary.
I was expanding the dimensions
From tip to toe in the daylight.
Not that myth of ghosts and terror
But arcane, deep
The night's fabric I became
Close to the fertile soil, I lay.
Eyes, ever-glowing stars that blink
And sigh to all who sleep
From behind the wall of confusion.

DIVERSE WEATHER

The westerly wind blows in the parapet
From the sky of cadavers, calx
And the horror
Of being entrapped in a battle wreck.
The wind sounds like a ghost cry
An ominous curse
From every slaughtered dream.

The easterly wind blows to my yard
Of a housewarming ceremony,
Of a birthday boom in candle sheen,
Of a new-born homecoming, the oath-taking
Of marriage in a joyous gathering
From a coloured centripetal canopy.

The northern wind blows toward me
From the devastation and despondencies
Bringing some dry leaf and queries
Of why tear the tender ties savagely
Why vices are being promoted
To afflict the society
Why the black umbrellas
Cover the mystery.

The wind is diverse and heavy
Over my gable, looms
In colossal disturbance
In my skull, I am raining needles
The agony of helpless haemorrhage.

AFAR, ELUSIVE

O life's beauty, the pristine face
How deep your sheen has drowned
Under the despair,
The despair of dying as weeds
What worse there could be.
How faded have you become
On the oppressive
Who is born of slavery
Bakes on the flame
And withers daily passing
Through the limbo of struggle.
O life's beauty, the pristine face
You are afar, apart, elusive
To the plain hands.
You are a wistful wound
In the bleeding heart.

From the royal terrace
Is grasped and seen
As a distant full moon
In the glorious sky, smirking
Or the pride reflection of it
On the glorious surface
Of the lake beneath.
O life's beauty, the pristine face.

CHILDHOOD

I have heard from them
Families got split, and their dwelling
Ousted the lineage of helpless grass
Now the living faces are like mildew.

The open space amidst the houses
Where the sky, wind, and children
Used to meet was wrested
More concrete walls to hide
More schemes.
Only the narrow road
In gloom leading to an uphill city.

Even those landmark trees
Abolished, no umbrella, all lay bare
The beauty, the babbling river
Is numb from the burning
Of the blisters on the bank.

Even the soil slope road
That used to take me home
In one breath
Has been filled with greed
And now is a flat plane.

Sparsely some bamboo bushes
Are left, perhaps, the ghosts
Are mourning on them
I am afraid to go, lest
I may not meet
My childhood soul.

EVENING

Amidst the quaint furniture, she
Waits like a moor to greet me.
Evening, the beguiling evening
Carries the embryo of the night
When the sun dips in the den.

She sneaks but does not leap
Till I spark the candle and
Burn some incense sticks: rose,
And sandalwood perfumed.

O, her face! Eruditely brightened,
Tungsten red; begirded by
The abyssal dark vineal greed.
A long pent-up constellation
Of passion starts pouring
Into my empty chalice inspiration
When my limbs rest on her rib.

I drink, drowning my mast to forget
Just an hour ago, I lost a day.

WINDOW

The door has concealed her
For many years.
The scattered pieces of the fancy vase
Broken by the gusty wind
Is not fixed yet.
The adventure doesn't
Trouble her feet anymore.
There, on the window frame-
She imagines a painting.
I, like a postman, bring the rays of hope
In the wrap of bread and milk, then peep in.
She cleans the dust
And pampers the glass, staring
At the street cat as time goes by.
She flips her hair, makes part in ways,
Press her lips, and check
If the dimple is in place!
Some sizzling chiffon slips from her chest
Then she curses: "damn to the beauty, damn the world,"

Still, she grows, now is growing like a scrawny vine
Over the years, her tongue forgets
The taste of wine.
The only truth she knows
Is the spring and the promise
I see her passion rises like a sea wave
Through the lonely parlour when the breeze blows
On her plain face once more,
Nature revives nature.

I WON'T MISS AGAIN

Even for the world's richest affair
I won't miss the rainfall again
O, that sound when it falls
On the parapet railing
Like a mallet on a xylophone, on even bits
The taps of the droplets' feet
My heartbeat, nostalgic
I will lose myself in that song
Again and again, forever
And be the drop, dance in a flow
And be free.

I won't miss the carefree giggle
On the rosy moisture lips,
Of the child again, that disproves
The notion of wretched, weary life
My heartbeat, nostalgic, on the even bits
I will lose myself, laugh lunatic
With the giggle in sync, play like a tambourine
With a jingle stick and be free.

Even for the world's richest affair
I won't miss again gazing
At the clustered cloud and dream,
As if I am floating like a swan on the surface
Of a still blue, and drift to the land
That invites me with love.

I give up the trial of question and answer
In the silent song of my heartbeat
I find my peace gliding in an abyss
Of if there's anything between the past
And the present and swing in an astral body.

SUMMER

I promised I would leave the rush and liaisons
And wait to hear the knock at the door
Of my weary heart that's longing to see you.
I will come to you and give all my time, endless
When the thick cloud will be furled and kept aside
And the sky will be a translucent plane, a lucid lake
Where sometimes the angels can be seen floating.
And the daylight will be kind to visit each house
And all the places around will have a golden glow
The newly grown soft fresh grass wayside, rich lushness
Will heal the yearlong stress of my poor vision
The body will feel the warmth of your closeness
And sweat in the urge of love and union
And chickweed, morning glory, and pansies will smile
And make me alive to be able to sing with them
And sweet-scented air will blow my hair and tease me
You will have me singular with you, and in silence
We will share each other's forlorn stories.

DRIZZLING AGAIN

Oh, it's drip drop
Drizzling again
In one breath, I sped
To the windowpane
And began humming
The old song: "pitter-patter
Falls the rain."

Aye, the soothing shower
Soaked the droughty soil
The lone wind whistling
For the farmer's ending toil.

The green Burdock, the creeper
And the grass turned glossy again,
Fringed with crystal drops,
They swayed in fain
The insects crowded
On top of the Dhutura cone
For they found there
The freshwater stored.

And suddenly, raining cats and dogs
Like a drum sounded in my head
All disappeared to find a shed
Was sky showing the anger then
Once was shower, then a flood
Once was glee, then a gloom
I spotted a floated boat
With a sail in wonder as 'why.'

CHAPTER - 3: WAKE

TRAGIC TUNE

The goose feather had fossilized.
I have been writing and writing
Gold, copper, and bronze age
Darker than the impending future is
The crude carbon resin ink.

A ball pen and my bent finger is
Noting on alabaster-snow mind paper
Some ornamented regret
Of abhorring hypocrisy, the wireless
Virtual civilization has wrought.

From the cornice of the conviction
The crippled hope is hanging.

I am bottled in the basement,
Striving to seize the rescue rope
Of the suspension bridge, coveted
If I could preserve the beauty, piety
And honesty of a man to a man

O traveller, don't play that sad tune
In lyre harp, that prod the old pain
Of the forgotten, disputed girl
Whose bare hands, appealing
Time and again: "Give me my sun,
Let me go beyond your notion,
For I bear the fruit for you".

O traveller, don't play that tragic tune
In lyre harp, that prod the old pain
The boy who lost the path of ascent
In the ammunition, anger turns insurgent
For one faithful breath in the air.

Many lyrics are being made, yet
The harp plays the skeleton scream
The beauty, piety, the honesty
Of a man to a man is still debasing
Over from the oceans and continents
The tragic tune never ends sailing.

VENTUROUS WORDS

In limitless directions
Those venturous words
Aimless, wings clipped
Absconding to a hideout
In alarmed sleep

How many times
In front of how many faces
The utterance stormed
Like flakes of philosophy
With balsamic beauty

Were never pealed
But was opposed and ruled out
By you, and your catalytic
Published notions
Of concurrent outlooks

And my extreme parlance
Of woods and streams
Of sweat and soil
Embraced drastic death
And became mummies
Beneath the service tray

Yet the rebellious pen
Breaks acrylic nails
While digging radical words
To question the cause
Of conspiracy, catastrophe.

I KNOW WHY

I know what you did yesterday
You, to climb up has built the turret
Between the sky and the sea
You, to leave a footprint, have dug
The secret of clone and collagen chemistry
You, to live to eternity has decoded
The alchemy of the honeybee
You, to impoverish the night, shackled
The arm of water and air, hence
The surmounted day has lingered:
Everyone struggles to sleep now,
For the continual beeping of microchip-memory
And your binary punched face on every wall
Flashing, a demagogue speaking.
You, so giant that one leg is in mine
And other in space-satellite
You tucked too much meal
That you could not deal with it
Your nuclear anger is a pillage
Of destruction, an intellectual game
And you said: "I did not do it."

Who did it? Who did it then?
I know why my epistle was tabled,
For you did not want to approve love
That will cease the war and conquer all.

DISTANCE INCREASING

In myriad complaints and distaste
Develops incessant enmity
I am drifting slowly to another planet
A slight crack in alacrity.

In the interim, the hands
Are slipped, the silence roars
In the gap between elliptic talks
Like skin-piercing shrieks
Of starved vultures and dogs

The distance is increasing
In physical and mental quanta
The distance is increasing...

Among your close association
Though my arrival is late
I am the fulcrum in theory.

The words, when exposed
To the air, explode as gunpowder
Hence unto the gyre of the world
I am pinching them with a pen.

Hark the finger's howl
See the fertile hand if you can!
From your inflamed ego
I am grappling at a meter distance
Give it a try, dear, give it a try!

I am shattering, shrinking gradually
Of despair, tears welling in the alley
The distance is increasing, increasing
As moving away afar, the galaxies.

THE PROMISE

The parley promise you made
At an altar of hunting time staid,
Even those with no lips
Listened to every word spoken
Seed sowed, weather downed and
The denial came with a season of famine.
But that broken promise holding on
To a bough of a cliff asking
A reason for abuse.

Only because of the elemental pledge:
That His cosmos breath
Shall travel all path through me
That the enthalpy of the burning vacuum
Shall rejuvenate my surfing spree
That His moistened eye
Shall open a fount of empathy
And His etheric body would
Reflect my sole integrity, was
The paramount faith with which
I walk on the desert's oasis.

Your chronic pain, jittery nerve
Is it not the cause
Of the guilt, deceit, and denial?
The virgin promise:
Like a road gives to a goer
Like a gardener gives to a flower
Received an unnatural death
That you erased like a scream in the dream
And you overruled all that was said.

FEAR

I could see the beaming spire
A colonnade to be built
For the pier, as a gate to the ocean.
When the spirit is awake
And rises to the peak
Then why does the fount
Dry to a drop!
From the Hades of my head
For the rivalry, a dark shadow
Like Cerberus grows colossal
And pulls me with the hairy hand
Like a bear's fishhook claws
To the darkness, darkness deep.
As if a stone, drops and ceases the light.
Fear- devours the possibility.
Naturally, I withdraw my feet.
It's a slim chance to cross
The line of fear, sharp like a blade.
The flood of thoughts devastating
Ruin the castle of dream
I wither as blossom, a life
Not full-grown, an apple no one sees

Collapse, a collapse to the brim
The blocks fall one by one,
Without a sword of faith, there
Remains nothing but
Fear is there, and fear is living.

BANAL EVENT

Under the roofless winter mist
And a miasma of angst, I stood shuffling
Blanket scarf to shield the infected tonsils
Entry denied being ten minutes early.
In the arena, the civilization was tall,
Gothic edifice and species of cars parked
And in the gap, hungry rooks were preening.
The bulk records of chronology, anthropogeny
Verified and signed after scrutiny but
My fingerprint was too faded; she
Suggested: "A drop of moisture would work."
Perhaps we qualified for our living place.
The man of sixty was still guarding
Our car for aid money as he handled
The parking, adjusting the garbage bin.
I felt for him, pronged. The sleek road
Looked like a stoneware dinner plate
And I wonder what he had in the dinner?
A dark age blacked me out while the car drove
On the home route, a chain of banal thoughts:

Life seems trash under the rich currency
And the cataclysm of mother earth consumes
Her nameless stepchildren invariably!

MILLIONS STARING

Perhaps living in ignorance
And unknowing is good.
From the peak of desire
You can buy pleasure and plunge.
Who is awake in the whole space
Of my head, stirring?
Millions starved, staring at my plate
While I am about to swallow.
Millions naked staring at my mind
While I am to buy the dress in vogue.
Millions in distress lift their hands
While I am to plan a trip one of a kind.
If you say life in pleasure is the only life
You have known; then I am dead
I don't know what I should do
To stop them from staring at me.
The mockery finally brought me
Down to the floor.
Don't give me a strange look
As I am slovenly now. I sleep
On the mattress peacefully.

21ST CENTURY

The posture of the facial trace
What eyes-lines-lips address
Is like reflections of seasons.
That cultured stomach, vitamin-rich
Legs of fortune resting for decades
Their attire, wolf's fur coat and
Trendy torso festive, yet the air is toxic.

Often their pale face fades
The ascending incentive day
As if broken, barren earth is bearing
A skeleton death mask.

Whenever he walks by me
Swaggering, I try hard to read-
The complex calligraphy
Where I see a famine face
Falling of the 21st century.

Yet the pristine beauty remains
In those pale furrowed race
Who has no questions but to destiny
A prayer for a truce with the crisis.

Their frozen eyes, natural mirror
Where no past or future is seen
Only the road extends far and far
Passing through the ribcage.

Always like a magnet, they draw me
To the scene, and I kept staring
For long till life and nature coalesce
I behold and the downing day smiled.

PARTING

They were parting
Feeling in their bone
The lethal pain.
Bleeding petals
Were all over the streets.
It might be the last meeting
Before the life battle began.
Eyes were penetrating, stilled
Forewarn uncertainty, and dread
Without vallum, roofless.
The teardrops defied the gravity
Froze on the shore
Of the barren city, yet
To the family, they affirmed:
"The universe has a bigger plan."
In the cracking cold
The warmth of the clasp
Was the last hope, last recall.

They witnessed the face of ruin
They bid Goodbye, moved on
To the path of destiny,
Gave a final kiss to which
They knew as life.

I SEE HIM RUNNING

I see him running, running
Wearing the muscle shield.
Morning and evening
On the same road where
Once life has been.
Is he burning the unabating stress
In salty sweat's stream
Or is he running away from the sign
Of death, that he felt
In the knee and nape, knocking!

I see them chatting
As if knitting an intriguing plot
For the play
Their gesture is but cynicism.
The shadow of the seasons
Slickly passes on over their head
What might they be talking about?
Are they sweeping the grief,
Exhuming the pain from the tomb,

Or trying to run away
From the solitude!
I've observed the fret
On their quivering brow.

CONVERSION

Over the way of my alcove glen
And there on the far shore
Of your whirled anxiety taking place
Many nuclear shifts irrespective
Of our disposition and dislike.

I gaze upon aphasic on affairs
Like a silent star from afar,
At the years-old Deodar, dying
And turning into the black cinder
In the ravenous flames of rancour.

And in venomous lust depravity
Human pulse losing chastity
They are spawning and burdening
Without having one apple a day.

The village does not take a heed
Of the erosion of alluvium but
Steadily the river is changing force.

The dangling girder bridge falls
On the mediocre hopes, cutting off
The nerves of the drone city.

It is hard to ascertain the cause
Of why hair cascades like the flakes
Of Delhi smog and the body-mass
Sustains on delirium and drug
And in the silhouette of your elite face
Is shining, only damnation and denial.

PENDULUM

Yes, I am living, fiddling
With my life and in my head
The old temple bell resounds
Till today on the hillock,
The anxiety of alteration
Ensuing in the wheel of time.

All those narrow roads,
A few relics and others are
Tucked by gossiping turf…
The tall oak, Deodar grew old
And Creeping Juniper leapt,
They know what would unfold
As the pendulum oscillates,
A change is taking place.

The indelible flaws
Aren't visible in Edison's filament,
The epidermis of Aphrodite
Worn as pampered beauty.

From my bone, the soggy fat
Tells a tale: a change is taking place
And I lament in the memory cassock
For my old town, and old man, lost.

FACE OF JOY

Throughout the spring when
The wind hums secret sonnets
To the mustard valley,
In the foothills, flowers sway
Tilting their head laterally
From right to left, left to right
In a rhythmic dancing feet
There my sight swoon and lean
On the palette of mustard yellow linen
It is then, a small grain
Of happy hormone I swallow
And climb on a phase higher
To yell, "what a joy!"

You, the gluttonous ruler
Did you swallow the same grain,
When you yelled, "what a joy!"?
After your attained victory
Over the weak opponent
You hoisted up the bloated flag
On the pyramid of corpses,
And your hallucinated head
Leaned on the linen of red blood
That I see on the face of joy.

STANDSTILL

The gruelling 'market collapse' recurs
Every decade with boulder grip,
Clueless, why we cannot bend it ever!
Among us, many who run a small savings
Inflicted by dogmatized despondencies they're.
What's this invisible predator's purpose here
Is it to disburden the earth, who conspire?
Apparently, we all are virtual, couched
And jammed within walls; it is no more a rumour.
The man who sweats to carry a family wagon,
Plots a probable graph of his fate, his ear
Glued on the blurted number of the TV screen.
Life comes to a standstill, no ripples seen
On the surface, aesthetically poetic as if a lake-body
With beauty sleeping, but irony, the difference
Is in conception between the lake and the life.

Few got protruded belly, and others got skinny
Under the stress of a whipping turbulence
Felt behind the door, and an abrupt heartbeat
But the woman in the kitchen standing diligent
As if absorbed by the wrap of infinite time
For a new recipe that would taste discrete.

CARE

Hardship is hoarse and hard, literally
Like a shard-laid path, true it is.

When imposed as fate by birth,
That bruise every wish you made
At the heel and heart, and many
Are dwelling in it.

The pain that pains the fibre
Of feelings, make you forlorn
And breaks the bone of living
But on the contrary
You sense and experience
How ruthless and excruciating
The painful state is to anyone.

Thus, will you stop inflicting
The rashes of derision, suffering
From the volcanic resentment
Of boasted self-esteem uppity?

None here born as master but all
Are honing to master the craftsmanship
Is it too difficult to empathize and admire?

Sometimes it seems all are busy
Hoarding their winter provisions like ants
Beware that you're not making a profit
Of your passion too desperately
Will take you nowhere other than
Reward you an exile glass wall of glory.

FAITHFUL

Think of Karna or even Josiah
In their heraldry of faithfulness
The alchemy of God can be seen
That's how you conquer a life
When the spark rule in your gene.

He stood firm, left leg numbed
Knee-deep trapped under
The thick ice of distress
Right leg lifted high on loyalty.

He thought of his beloved
Ere the bullets pierced his chest.
Her wet hair tickled his nape
Her simple smile, romantic drip
One last time he kissed in the air…

The first bullet: punctured hopes
He pulled a heavy breath and felt
Two lithe hands curled
Around his grief, it was his son
Who whispered two love words.

He couldn't pull the trigger
At the enemy, having foreknown
The trauma of his family and keen.

He preferred to be martyred
For loyalty and faithfulness to mercy.
In existence, he is one of a kind
Having countless bullets in his life
He remained forever in my mind.

VALENCE

In life, what we plan to be
And what we become is mere a chance.
And how we work on the surface is
What we feel as the valence of living.
Mostly they end up in the convoy
Of memoirs, constant conflicts
Absurdly placed in the alley
Between the head and heart.

When I wanted to be in the audience
I became a performer on stage
And was inharmonious.

The encyclopaedia made me hungry
Hence, I nibbled on vintage pages
Of thousand minds, indifferent.

I search for an answer
By looking up to the sky all day.
The first interview in that glass-built office
Surveyed well, but the host
Didn't like my face.

No matter what word you put to rejection
It always sounds rude, meant to crush all credit.
I ate cashew, felt fancy outfits on my skin
I did experimental travel and discovery,
Did that turn my gene elite?

A plebeian who breaks down
On the streets on every corner
Looking at a beggar and a benighted.

The excess always flows against the river
Bizarre, where we are, we never wanted.

HISTORY REPEATS

One more year went past thinking…
Rewarded lives of knighthood
Finally asleep, under the red soil
Yearning for the golden time, one more year
Was gone from my grip, another
Came waving as a cycle.

The season with a persuasion
Of the bright sun on my windowpane
Brightens the contrast of the vision
Moors are back in jade green.

The stiff joints and jinks are
Recovered buoyant and pliant again.
The elm and oak seem budding
And the drifted bird returning
Under the full-grown canopy,
The fledglings seek a clear sky.

The melted ice revives the river,
The river revives the city plane
But the evil remains an evil villain
Whipping more hate and greed.

The big heads, diplomats wrapped
By the big banners of NATO peace
Innocent killing makes a victory
It is the Sovereignty and servitude
That history repeats, looming war smoke
Over the countries agreed on peace
One more year, I am still thinking.

WASH AWAY

The explosion bursts the starlit sheet
Of the civilians drowned in the dream of love
War, isn't war an expensive game!
Who produces weapons, and why? The message
Of peace is fluttering in the flag.
It's like tobacco and drugs.
You can get it easily if you want to...
See the warning: "Injurious to Health."
Some intangible words make my mind restless.
Black Market, Dark Web, Cryptocurrency -
Who are they, and why are their roots growing?
A few months ago, the child who was born
In many virtues, as a human being
Doesn't understand-
The face and mask are not one
The earth is spherical or flat
Only knows the shape of the mother's face.
Why is the mother's chest traumatized!
There is no smile on her face.
He cries, and the mother cries.

I cry, dark day and night.
So much crying! Won't so much water
Wash away the egoism and aggression
Of the extreme world!

WANT PEACE

How can I practice remaining in silence
When there's a beastly drumbeat
Striking in the chest?
The timber of conviction, rot by termite
Is breaking like a jute stick, no remedy.

The aggression of the powerful
The fear of the weak
The terror of war
Is the history and the future.

Socialism-imperialism-capitalism
How many more palaver!
In the round table outpouring,
Fermented liquor.

Whose possession is the space
Between the perimeters! Bellows
Friction and faction and
Conflicts undefined.

A folk of young stork was seen

With books of technology-medicine-economics, future sky.

Today they are dressed in the decree of death,

Sten gun in their hand; with their bone

And bone marrow, gallon blood, will protect

The interest and base of the country.

Let the bridge break, let the structure collapse,

Let the edifice fall; It will be rebuilt

What's in that?

How will you return the orphaned

And the broken child's mother's soul

By oath, the birth of the father

Is for the country, or else life is futile.

It's not too late yet

From the Indus to the Nile, the fire

Of aggression is flaming forth

Only those who think of the world

They want peace; I want peace.

ALARM

The animals fight each other
By instinct for food.
Man is sent with infinite wit
And a perceptive heart with lenity.
By testament, they can create profuse
If the necessity arises, and
Their fight is against calamity.
If man contrives to fight to harm and injure
They are no longer a man, a half-man
With a demon-head. A red alarm
For an imminent terror of annihilation.

LET US LIVE

Come, my brothers, sisters
Of the world, at one place, rational.
Under the persecuted sky,
And on the grieving soil,
Let us breathe, the coiled air
Of the last decade and ask each other
What do you feel all day? Putrid and pungent?
The smoke of the gunpowder,
The covert corpse in the trench
The flame of ruinous obstinacy,
Digging all roads, hell-bound.
Is there any piety left of the primal air?
Each coat of conspiracy
Can be felt in bodily anxiety.
Don't sleep tight further, thinking,
Someone else is a victim.
Can the mother earth drink
The shed blood of her child, no, no, can't be.

It goes to the red sea; in my throat, there
The water is brackish and bitter.
They're together, a cohort, where are we!
Hold my hand, dear friends
Let us make a footbridge, unruled
From the Arctic to Antarctica,
And our slogan will be, "One life, Let us live."

TILL THE WAR IS OVER

I know, I know, how terrorizing
The frequent air raid sirens are.
Run, run, find a dungeon subway, hide
Or cross the border, be nameless,
Be a refugee, save the life, you
Are not a coward, saving a life.
She doesn't know where your father is
O child, sleep, help your cloven mother
Sleep. Till the war is over.
There is no more terrible disease than war.
Filth is fine. Sanitization is an old concept.
You will eat one bread sharing among
The rats, the dogs, and the germs together
You will live till the war is over.
O, soldier! I salute your bravery!
Remember, if you die fighting
Sacrifice your last drop of blood,
We will honour your name in heraldry,
And rejoice in the victory
Commemorating you.

THE MEANING OF MY POETRY

How man grows and dries
Like the green leaves,
And rest together
In the same grave, perhaps
I have been writing that
With nuanced emotions.
I share the same sun throughout,
Lying beneath the foil of affair with them.
Sometimes it is a complex texture
Sometimes it does not rhyme
But it is the life of poetry
Ends as a cycle from its source.
If a reader chooses to raft
In the current of the poem
The taste lingers in him as one.
The idea that develops from the reflection
In the eyes, and becomes
A pulse to the nerve, affirms
In the brain as perception is private.
Hence, your remark doesn't upset me.

The words my poem illuminates

Maybe ancient yet pertinent

To my parading thought.

My poetry which only paddles hope

Can never scream

To draw your attention

Rather they will rest on the pages

The safest place I built for them.

The words will make a necklace

Of honour to them who see no distinction

Between a bird's tweet and a man's cry

Who understands that the agony, affliction

Is the ocean of realization, where

A man can wake in the light of life.

NO WORD

I have received the news
Your loved one took a flight to the ether
Beyond the clouds, left you forever
To ache in this secret cave alone.
The scar won't heal, but a new skin
Would appear to mask it from the people.
I searched for a word to console in vain
For there seems no such word
By which I may close the vacuum.
And the words which come on my lips
Glorifies death over agonized life,
Wouldn't that be an affliction to the bereft!
On the funeral march, my leg won't move
Or stand by the crematory wharf,
For I don't have the word in my mourning soul
To shroud your grief, forgive me!
Forgive me that I didn't say a word.

HEARSAY

The common hearsay "Age is a number,"
Is hackneyed.
Do you ever hold the age in your hand,
To measure its meaning and depth?
Is it a number or a stair?
You are climbing step by step
And in the final tread, all is empty
And a heap of regret.

Had you known that
Every talk is deeper than the sea
You would have seen those Teak trees
Turned strong and bold,
That was planted three centuries ago,
By your great grandfather
Now demands the attention of all
As it sways its leaf.

You would have seen two more generations
Following you from behind,
With an inevitable demand whispering:
"You had brought enough grey.
Leave the stage. To fly, we need space.
We will break, we will create,
We are the young angels of the architect,
Leave the stage."

BURDEN

The burden of the century, as if
I had born a thousand times with hope
Taking an oath in the surge of waves,
Carrying like a coachman, the nuisance
Done by my brethren and me.
Not repaired, not corrected, left
As collateral damage, an old scar.
The weight frescoed on my spine
Is too heavy; it has crouched my body.
O fie! Why do I write! True justice,
Honour, and service are only the ideology
Equality, of what? Will live in utopia.
Your victory over my defeat is all a farce
The world will be ruled by avarice.

YOURS AND MINE

What is there in a name,
And grotesque sentimentality
Only ruins future proximity!

My companion, come hither
Tell me if you see the disparity
In the essence
Of rose and red blood
Of fire and desire
Of love and care.

Somewhere unites,
The blue sky, akin
How to distinguish yours and mine
Into the stretches of blue hues
I blend and see the birds
And the souls are free.

The soil smells the same
Yours and mine
Like the clothing and balsam
Of the mother's body
That holds the roots of life
Turns into a soft bed
In the final sleep.

In one earth distance, divided,
Building home, you, and me?

NATURE OF MAN

I have had joy in its zenith
Through the butterfly senses
Till it lost the odour of ecstasy.

I have broken the frame
Of the firefly fantasy
Stumbling on ordeals
And waking into reality.

I have observed for years in silence
About nature in its naturality.

I have known the alchemy
Through the search for why:
The water cascades
Flower blooms
The fire burns
The oyster holds the pearl
And the chameleon walks
In camouflage…

Only the man's nature-
I never comprehend,
Who Break, mend and break again
Abides by no laws.
The abruptness, the aberration
Forever creates a division
Between my path and yours
Between man and the mind.

GRACE

Come in millions, armed with
Missiles and tanks of wrath.
You may crush me with fragments
Of emotion. Yet you will see
A bold head erectly holding,
Invariably emitting photons instead.

And the cosmos of your eyes
Is the same cosmos that dies
And is reborn in me each day
With chasmic grace.

Hear my breath, is singing…
For all your envy and hate
There will be a poesy of red rose
For all your enmity and rage
There will be a love upstage.

To welcome you at the door
I will spread the empathy petals
All over, like carpet on the floor
Irrespective of your stance.

CHAPTER – 4: LIVE AND LOVE

TAKE IT, BE IT, AND SPREAD IT

I am one of the stars, like you.
The disparity of palates and speech
Formed continental span
Between the two, yet I love you
And you wonder, how I do?
For I have a harpoon foresight
That led me to cipher matters
From zero to absolute
Even in no moon solitude

My wrinkled eyes look at you
Through the concave glass
But a clairvoyant sun,
In my frontal lobe can plunge
And perceive the seashell brain
And I know why they frowned at me.

Do you know, last time
From filthy fly reeds rodent road
When I was heading on the highway
They slammed the door on me
And I knew, through the fissure
They frowned at me!
Then hoisting my feet on my
Headstrong eagle wings, I flew
Beyond sleep, wake, and dream

They never saw me
Nowhere near any temple altar
They bluntly said: " She has no religion!"
You know-
I never mind! I never frowned!

Up to the summit and down
To the valley, my journey
On the nomadic path taught me
How love breathes on the membranes
Of fern, mushrooms, and parsley
Amidst the oak and pines,
Origin of love lights on me,
I give you but that light, take it,
Be it and spread it on your field.

ANOTHER IMITATION

Why, why I walk again,
Having been parted from you
In that impassable path
Though I know
Those dispersed seeds
Of you, of the subtle being,
Will haunt me.

From the supernal sea
In the uterine, I emerge
The jubilation of the earth
For another imitation
Which begets time
And again, the infirmity,
Senility, and death.

Why so much honey
In the parting tune
Hence, I come to depart
Again, and again.
Only love...and love
What else is there to seek!
My growing tendrils hold on
To the pillars of Kinship.

Within my skeleton cage
I am a captive bird
O, bondage! Unleash me.
Why is the gravity dragging
Me down, even when I am
Rising beyond the horizon!

THEY BLOOM

They bloom in geometry
On my bosom's boulevard
By drinking the extract
Of my generous love mist

Their canopy spreads wings
Limitless unto my bountiful sky
Like streaming morn rays

Their taproots drill deep
Into the soil of my soul
Like a Shephard tree
In the parched land

Family: a compact, cubic kin
Surrounds a cerulean fallacy.

When they break and bust
In autumn, my spring fades
Yet when those hands depart,
I do not remain fertile-
And full in my elemental clay!

O, heart! Spare my soul.

Don't let me be desert devoid of moisture.

Let the bliss flow to eternity

For I am still his, whom I belong.

MY MOMENTUM

My metal determination
Did not melt,
In the coulter of sweat labour.
My liquid thought did not condense
In the heathenish treatment
Of the reaper.
In all states of matter, I claim
To exist in the spiral galaxy-arm.

I bring the momentum
By worshipping the origin,
In my nebula pillars.

Rejuvenated omnipotence, running
In my veins and sinews madden me
To be creative in hues amidst the fall.

When on the country rail
The Kash Phool coats me
By terracotta ambrosia flavour
My heart dances in merriment
To the rhythmic beat
Of the ascending day
Invariably
On a rainy day
On a sunny day
Even on an unnamed day
Where my days dress up
In the theme of life
For a divine celebration.

THINKING OF YOU

Yet your yellow torpid body
Like the grown country grain
In the epoch and age spurs
Long-ignored senses.

Yet your trembling breath
Like the catalytic wave of hope
Yields liberal love strokes
As the white Gardenia
On leafy growth.

Yet your thermic touch
Transmits the same degree of warmth
My impetus and your impulse
Alas! A leap year it was,
When you mirrored my face.

We garnered many reaped seasons
Now, words are unnecessary
When our silence speaks-
Debate and reasoning
Turn pale and bleak.
And I win by winning you
And I fail by defeating you
There is--

No game in between.

FREEDOM ECSTACY

Perhaps they felt freedom
Who marched on martyr's blood
And sacrificed self
Freed the chained people
From slavery, and reinstated
The right of the country.

I don't possess Albatross wings
To disburden my distress and fly high
I cannot dart in rocket speed
To set a journey beyond the sky.
Can I know of freedom ecstasy?

Whenever I dare to utter
What I have known as truth
Through nature and nurture
Being gallant, my heart blasts.

Words for justice
Break boundaries, regardless
Of ramifications
Like water-reservoir floods.

My free soul liberates
From all bondage
Of corrupt laws, myth, and stigma
In that momentary life-battle
My tongue tastes the freedom.

BELIEVE IF YOU CAN

Leaning on a puddle of fog,
I ponder the events harping
The doubts provoke apprehensions
But a high current that speaks
In my head: believe,
Believe in what you conceive
If you are to see the life
With sensation as mauve.

It is the belief of waking up
As a lump of restored clay
That let me sleep like an unborn foetus
It is the belief that death is far, far away
Let me live like all the heyday
It is the belief that we all are
The alike souls as the body of the cosmos
That let me wreathe and cling unto you

Though at times, the dropped coin
On my palm, betrayed showing
A tail of foul fate, and I lose a limb,
Life on the crutch, ascertain
But the belief resurrected again
As new cells in the body
Nothing but an incredible parody.

It was never hard to choose
An untrodden path among many
Straddled with the certitude of hope,
And doubt never show up in the vicinity
I walk in the nature where
The sun smiles, the moon ascends
The wind titillates in gratitude
For believing in them.

REALIZATION

I was forlorn searching
You in all the forest of faces
Being known, your dwelling
Somewhere
In their inner cognizance
But they all were creeping
With crab legs on the shore of shining
And were shooting judgment bullets
For the survival of the fittest.
Each step I took back, I realized
A piece of coal, and a diamond crystal
Aren't the same thing
I crouched down into the conch shell
And settled under the sea
Within the quiet breast
Of my profound being there
I found you, absorbed
Perforating in corals body.

IMAGINE

Imagine:
A river is coming down
As a slithering serpent from the sky.
A cloud is sometimes shifting
As a white Pegasus or cotton candy.
A tree is standing like a watchman
With bushy green hair.
And the wild animals
Are guarding you as the clan.
A snowflake is dancing like a fairy.
A day is a royal carpet
On which you walk
Like a king or a queen.

See, on your lips
Return the long-lost grin.

Your life will regain those
Necessary supplements
If you lighten your head for a while.

Fantasies are sometimes precious
To flatten failure and squalid grief.

When we have nothing to embellish,
Fertile imagination
Is a bestowed boon.

The captain once used it
As a life force to steer the ship
Towards an unseen treasured land
Got over the tempest
And landed safely.

UNEXCAVATED POETRY

The red cells were gushing
Fiercely through the veins
She could've been a Redwood
Standing skyward, infinitely resolute
The outburst of adverse emotions
And varying viewpoints
Made her fall like the chaff bud
Of a mango tree
On the embankment of the gully.

The vitality of the sizzling sun
Was surging within the third eye,
She could've glowed like the brightest star
As Sirius floating skyward, infinitely resolute
The lack of courage to bear any collapse,
Made her fall like a forgotten meteor
Lost in the isolated crater.

The heart exhibited a lagoon
Of trust, and a sea of empathy
She could've lived in the full measure
Of a sapience being
But in the tussle of judgment
On the page of destiny
She remained unexcavated poetry.

UNCOMPROMISING

The world says pink is my colour
I don't put it on, for it causes
Vulnerability in the body and mind.
The cloak, 'woman'...
Do you think it is all rosy?
I accepted-
Thrown stormy-stony challenge
I lacked breath-
Clambering the trough and crest
I fought hard with stern muscle
Aching, bleeding cyclical in my flesh.
Shed tears to moisture my wound
Till my eyes were numbed and dried.
Fractured each part of my being
Till I found no sentiment has cared.
Today I say it was all worthy
Accepting life and its multi-shades
I came out stronger, bolder, tall
In a journey uncompromising.

I LOVE LIFE

When my eyes see
The sapphire glow in your eyes
And the wintry path
That leads to my house
Covered with the blooms
Of genial April,
I love my life.
When my nerve pulsates
In the Ganges' spirit
And I irrigate a sterile life
Love finds its way
To ensure
The virtue of life.
When my life dawns
In the dale, woken by sunlight
And in a trailing shadow of the night
Reflects the choices made, life in
Conflicts, concur, calamity

Draws a circle
I see the cordage of air
To the being
How worthy and adorable
Life is at play
O, death! Heaven's decree-
Delay, delay…

PROPHECY

I wake hours and days
Listening to the voice of the sages
That echo: foster the best
Bestowed upon you.

After the lapse of thousand years
We hear the prophecy again
Prophecy, as the hymns of flower
Through the meadows of the centuries
From every compass.

From the sacred sanctuary
The shadow of the oracle raises
The humanity, to unite, to revive
For the accord and peace.

Within the wrap of modernism
I still see that a soul primitive, lives
Hence, I call my brethren
Come together in ally
Let's hoe and weed the ground
To sow and reap a new era
To worship and honour the wizard
For the Creator expresses
The virtue of the creation
Through skill, wit, and the art of man.

ANOTHER YEAR

Precisely 365 days, one whole year
With a meticulous memorandum,
I clutched unto the Aspen and Poplar
For a year of revolution. The earth's
Spine burdened more than before,
Yet deflect not even by an inch
From the compass of obligation
See, I returned to my planetarium.
In the list of do's and don'ts
Bizarre images of ogres and elves
Wasn't the harvested fruit as wished
The thin hair fatigue fancy ascribes
The tongue and taste changed a bit.
Today on a clean slate, I write a rebirth
Milk thought, heart angelic, intent purity
To exalt as grace in the eyes of divinity.

JOY

When the bees quaff the nectar
Lingering on luscious lavender,
When the orphaned child earns
The bounty on the temple's tribune,
When the camel soaks the throat
From the first drizzle of the desert,
-they're tucked by joy and sink.

The two perennial pink blossoms
On the joy wheel, body-fixed
Fear-frozen, like the Mustang
Galloping towards the final line
Their head leaned back in freedom
Lungs were fleeting as cotton
Their welded laugh spewed sparks
That permeated the black hole
They're tucked by joy and sunk.
And the joy kissed their soul, lip lock
To extoll the virtue of living in joy.

ALONE

There were bees and birds around
When days floated on golden rays
And night draped by soaring dreams
Swooning savoury was the evening
With an oriental dish and sugary flakes.

The years wilted youth into grey
Then talks were grave, empty foyer
Even the wind failed to keep ever
The nature green and gone astray.

I walked being ostracized, alone
Drifted on the road paved with stone
Waded on a hobbling boat, met
Real demon, with wavering hope.

I disavow not my scrupulous goad
That made me lonely, but not alone
My clematis companion with whom I live
Who can't be seen, shown, or be told.

LOVE SPEAKS

I no longer insist on him
To tell me, "Love you, darling."
His satire in Bollywood style irks me
To the extreme that I crack
A walnut between my teeth.

To become a giver, how much he must give
He is ignorant of that philosophy
Eighteen years of living together,
And he transformed into an ethereal
Gossamer shadow of my being.

I measure the salt or sugar
And his regular heartbeat.
Action movies may shoot up
The adrenaline, now he enjoys with me
The black and white of the '60s.

He has no craving, no desire other than
Seeing me smiling and breathing fine.
Through his silence, I learned love is:
A submission to imbecility, less logic,
And more acceptance of emotional instinct.

If by the decree of destiny,
He stays alone
When I will be gone, through nature
And neighbour, he would be happening.
His spirit of living would be waning
A thorn of guilt like mucus
Chokes me, and I tell him:
You mustn't forget yourself,
With all bestowed ability
You are living and breathing fine.

TOGETHER

I talk of lemon's freshness and literature
You talk of the changing map, China, America.
We both listen with a different sensibility.
My senses are sincerely taut yet soft,
You rest in the distant oracle, your mind.
Sometimes we are as silent as noon
And the river of time flows
Through us without a stumbling block.
Trains of thoughts moving forward arbitrarily, speeding.
Froths of opinions are ready for an impact.
We don't deny the unseen force called love
Exists and binds all matters. Naturally
Two parallel railroads carry lives
To the destination as promised precisely.

DON'T REST

No matter how tall a monument
You are, or a strong mountain…
Grief breaks you into the dust of grain.
And you look up to the emptiness
For someone to feel your heart.
Our experience has two facets
Thing to nothing,
And the transit is ever suffering.
That doesn't last long, do pass in rotation.
Haunting nights and stolid days
Do pass in rotation
And the Sun shows the God's face
When it awakes life, from under the sea
Above the soil, and in the soul.
Brighter than the golden rays
Emerge from abyssal opaque darkness,
The God's face, salient on sunny days.
Look yonder, higher, eager
Till the conundrum is clear and addressed
Follow the fire in the eyes, don't rest.

ONE DAY, YOU REALISE

Are you delusive, maybe
Confined within the maze of fancy?
She loves it if you pamper her hair.

One day, you may take her
To the open wide vineal roof
And show the full white moon
For a metaphor and tell
The mesmerizing beauty she owns.

One day, you may take her
To the remote, secluded stream
For a simile, and tell
The tribal serenity she owns.

One day, you will sit her
In the drowning light, with a
Hyperbolic wish, and drown smoothly
Into the depth of her breast. One day.

A feeling has no figure, no matter
What imagery you draw, it never arrives
There as you thought it to be
As if numerous gusty waves
Rise, fall, veiled, and rebel, then extinguish.

Once, try to feel her concrete,
Put no diction, however deep
Don't think any props whatsoever
See how far the wave travels.

A PROTOTYPE

They are a prototype, not a gender
In whose heart a secret trove
Of sparks weave and rise
Wait in ambush
To hook the dream.
Their will is, like a falcon, captive
Enabled for a potent flight, at times
The wings flitter flutter, then close
Looking for a beacon to guide
To a friendly place, a friendly page
To draw a persuasive design.
A gust of passion breaks
The hard crust anyway,
Then the urge
With an avalanche-force
Arrives in the lame lane,
Lit up the lamps for many
And they see a road ahead
To walk along with a smile
That removes the shadow
From those faces.

I FETCH

I never lack the fuel
That ignites the fire
To venture into something anew
But the search remains
For one on which
My soul floats blissfully.
The next pillar, not so far, I try
Into a deep forest, I go in trying
And stand on the tip of the needle
Lifeless like a dead tree-
In the middle of nothing.
No moon, or star, not a leaf
Not a smell of subject, no light
There's no way out or in, still.
Yet, I wish to be there
Again, again and again,
Day and night, even quarter,
Now and then, I paddle
To the hidden womb of stillness
To fetch a healing word for you.

I LIVE IN BETWEEN

From the dawn to the day
From the dusk to the night
Dawn and dusk, the doors
From where the sun enters
With benefaction and departs
Ceasing the light, a shift to clarity
From unknown, obscurity.

Between the two, like a snail
Within a brittle shell
Living with soft emotion
A domestic in the morning,
By the afternoon
A bohemian, I cruise blithe
In the cloud with a purple fairy.

Add, subtract, multiply and sigh
If not, then divide
And do reverse and sigh,
Mathematics doesn't have feelings.
Come one day by surprise,
And I'll be there scribbling
On the roof. On the floor
The lizards, silverfish, and others
Are happy all evolving,
There's no defined territory.

LET THE LONGING BE

Let the longing be, let it be.
Within the conch shell
Let it hark the sign and abide silently.
Let the thousand ocean waves
Being the humid air, storm, and gush
On the batten of the breast
See the breath is longing.
Life goes on with the sequence
Of flowers and thorns, holding the rudder.
The longing of the water to flow
Downhill from the mountain top
The longing of the vapour to take
A flight up from the water drop
The longing of her to him, actual to dream
Gradually lead the man as nature
To the threshold, eyes, mind, and meditation
Yet there remains the voltage of longing.
Someday, the shroud of longing succeeds
The edge of one sky, and flares up
Billion skies from the edge, further as longing.
The body is longing, sustained in longing.

SOMETHING HAS CHANGED

This is how turning flipping the daily grains
And blotted sheets, I reached the forties.
I walk along the arch of the day
To meet life eye to eye.
We sit in intimacy, wrapped
By the two corners of the decade quilt,
A utile dialogue that installs.

Life asks, following the ledger:
"Why did you choose to be right
At the cost of peace?
Go and get the cracked pieces
From the old crossing."

I seek that small skipping stone
Thrown playfully,
Which turned into a hazard.
Still stranded in the maze water.

Something has changed these days
The grief is glowing in the candle wick,
The frustration is in a phase
Of transformation, as melting wax.

In between, through the open, the envious stars
From a clear sky peer
Flashy evenings of the grand century
Tide and ebb
People must have knocked at my door
I don't know who came and went
When life and I, face to face,
The aura binds life to the soul
I know, the whole world
Around us even then does roll.

BE PLIANT

One finds the purpose of life in love
The hardest test is to let that love leave.
The blow of parting is a vortex
As if you let your 'soul' part into particles
And constantly ache of damnation
As if you let your breath die of constriction
As if the fact of losing ceases hunger
As if the light only brings shame,
And the darkroom is the only niche
Still, you have no choice
But to let it happen.

Let him go if he asks to be free
Let her go if she asks to be free
Ultimately, we realize
When it is time, we're inert,
Our most loved body go
For our soul to be free, this is truth.

To the galactic year, each life is a season
And the season comes to turn you green
Flower in fulfilment and seasons go.

Can you hold, possess, and bind things
When in the cosmos, things dissipate
From compaction in the direction of flow?
Try, try hard to open your thoughts,
Be pliant, be in motion and flow.

IT IS NOT A POMP

Don't ask me why I do, had you spent
One day in the grass field with me
Giving the key to your heart
I could show you; it's all true.
Do you think it's pomp? Only heaven knows
Why I adore you, but it's true
Each word I spell would be doubted,
Be mocked by the doomsayer and sceptics
Yet I want them to be read and transmit
Let me tell you, it's true.
You see on gigs how I laugh like a kid
And forget that I am hurt on my root
That I bring the sweet cake as delight and you
Are frightened of the theorized sharp edge.
I break as teary rain on arid stead
Yet deter not to imagine a smile on distressed.
History says every radical thought
Would be ignored, objected to, and hit by stones
At least it would penetrate a few heads
Parch and prevail on a path uncrowded.

A DOOR

She asked me then: "Now that as you seem
To take the flag forward,
What is your intention if I may ask?"
I quite mumbled, pendulous, and then gathered
Some strewn verbiage and spoke forth
In a flow: the earth has indebted me
To each cell of my body, like a bough bearing fruits
My head is bowed but in extreme gratitude
My feet bother, being too heavy on its chest.
The grain, the air, the sky, and the skull
All its mercy, the worth of my blood, my loyalty.
I ponder, muse with a few jingling coins in my
wallet!
What do I have, to offer you?
I would not hear the dystopian scream, squeal
To be assertive that they are all deprived
Of the wealth of love or lineage!
For I have known a door that opens to the infinity.
What is amiss? They are forlorn because
None can hold in each pixel-thought
The 5000 years of developing history.

I kneel on my knee for them to climb, a handful
Of abundance they may reap smiling,
But they will never see me standing nowhere.

I REGRET, I AM LATE

I write from the traces
Of my imagination, about
The magnificence of the dawn
I met the aflame aura close
On the other side of the vision
Standing once on the peak
Of the Tiger Hill
Such power play of light,
And the world is being pulled up
By the Sun in coherence,
Above the horizon
From the depth of dormancy.

I rise late when the day is
Above the quarter
Immemorial of the origin
I have known
Of how the world descends
To the darkness, powerless
And mourn without
The universal beacon.

There are many
Who never experience peace
And inner beauty that passes
I come across them
In the crowd, so close
To turn the pages
Of their heart, in oblivion
I have read all their written verses
That bleed the virulent and pernicious hatred
And I regret I am late; I could have woken up
Once in their hidden prison
Where the love is hibernating
To open the door to light.

I HAVE KNOWN THE PATH

Win or lose, don't be afraid.
Trying can show either of the two faces.
I have known through failure,
That win is not on the probability
But on the tenacity of trying.

I am not worried about the failure
Though it is dismal to be failed.
I am not afraid of the artifice
Though it is stinging to be cheated.

I have not even an iota
Of restlessness or doubt
In my thought, and moves
For it's like
I have known the path
To be walked long before.

I wake up each day with
A spirit to tilling a garden of scope
I listen to the potent with hope
As they would help plough the barren soil
And to believe is the first step
To set forth a plan
For as it said, few will be sent
With discreet wealth and power
And few will give hands, and altogether
They can share the burden
And wash away the pain.

I serve my part by kindling a lamp
That fulfils my heart
I am the temple and my thought
My word, my action is my karma
The true offering to the living God
And I feel by each day,
The spirit is expanding its wings
Soon it will be out of the cage
Of mortal sufferings.

EVERYDAY

I go to the crowd, gathering a few
Angularities of life and livelihood,
Emptying the pot
Some auxiliary talks, I pour
Somewhere life might flourish fully.
A speaker in grey cloth, giving
A bland discourse to the noise...
Lost in the crowd of thousands every day.
The crowd goes upward, a trade
On full business, and you know the counterfeit
Standing still, I search for the impetus
Like a small oyster in my palm is 'I'
Whose name etched, 'unparalleled.'
In your letter written, 'trust,' with that
I move forward amidst the ambushed deceiver
I come back again with an infant mind
Where the year is standing still, yet
After the evening, I glow up diminutive
In your vast sky, in adoration.

IN THIS LIFE

In this life, on the curtain
of my eyes
appeared lively earth
on the lap of a radiating sun
in the sky embellished
with glittery stars.

In this life, I have known myself
in my one etched name
and I have written that name
with fondness and pride
again, and again.

In this life, I have built a home
with the thread of many dreams
and dressed in many forms
and I have stuffed responsibilities
in the folds of my head.

I have played and acted
devoutly in love
there's no lack and flaw in any attempt
and I could see I had wrought
an inspiring epic in the battle of life
and fought bravely as a warrior
and the wounds washed away
by the rill of tears, I shed.

I never knew there was a life
before I was born
but I know as clear as my breath
there is an impending death
and I wish to say
I lived one whole universe through my eyes
now, I am ready to go...
But I fear, I fear to cut the cords of the bondage
that wrapped me so tight.

O dear God, promise me,
you will show your indefinable face
on the face of death, that would
keep my head high
when I must cross the transit of death.

END

CPSIA information can be obtained
at www.ICGtesting.com
Printed in the USA
LVHW081540080922
727696LV00012B/671